Song Book

Play Recorder Today! Songbook

Featuring 10 Rock & Pop Favorites!

ISBN 978-1-4234-8504-9

HAL•LEONARD® CORPORATION

7777 W. BLUEMOUND RD. P.O. BOX 13819 MILWAUKEE, WI 53213

Visit Hal Leonard Online at
www.halleonard.com

Introduction

Welcome to the *Recorder Songbook*. This book includes 10 well-known rock and pop favorites, and is intended for the beginner to intermediate player.

The songs in this book are carefully coordinated with the skills introduced throughout the *Play Recorder Today!* method. Refer to the right column in the table of contents below to see where each song fits within the method, and to help you determine when you're ready to play it.

Contents

About the CD

A full-band recording of each song in the book is included on the CD, so you can hear how it sounds and play along when you're ready. Each example is preceded by one or two measures of "clicks" to indicate the tempo and meter.

The CD is playable on any CD player, and is also enhanced so Mac and PC users can adjust the recording to any tempo without changing the pitch!

Track 1

Love Me Tender

RECORDER

Words and Music by ELVIS PRESLEY
and VERA MATSON

La Bamba

Track 2

RECORDER

By RITCHIE VALENS

Moderate Latin beat

* Count 3 measures of whole rests.

Track 3

What the World Needs Now Is Love

RECORDER

Lyric by HAL DAVID
Music by BURT BACHARACH

Moderate Jazz Waltz

3*

* Count 3 measures of whole rests.

Can You Feel the Love Tonight

from Walt Disney Pictures' THE LION KING

RECORDER

Music by ELTON JOHN
Lyrics by TIM RICE

Count 8 measures of whole rests.

Track 5

My Heart Will Go On

(Love Theme from 'Titanic')

from the Paramount and Twentieth Century Fox Motion Picture TITANIC

RECORDER

Music by JAMES HORNER
Lyric by WILL JENNINGS

Moderately

*

* *Count 8 measures of whole rests.*

Track 6

Eight Days a Week

RECORDER

Words and Music by JOHN LENNON
and PAUL McCARTNEY

How to Save a Life

Track 7

RECORDER

Words and Music by JOSEPH KING
and ISAAC SLADE

Free Fallin'

Track 8

RECORDER

Words and Music by TOM PETTY
and JEFF LYNNE

Moderate Rock

Lean on Me

Track 9

RECORDER

Words and Music by
BILL WITHERS

New note: C
(refer to fingering chart on page 15)

Hound Dog

Track 10

RECORDER

Words and Music by JERRY LEIBER
and MIKE STOLLER

Soprano Recorder
Fingering Chart

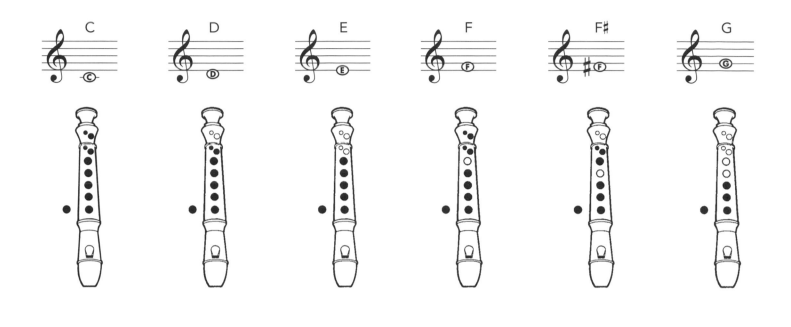

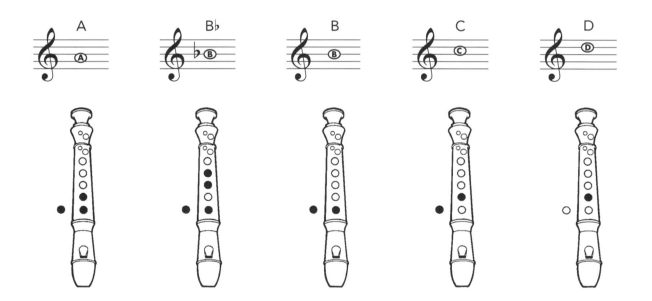

PLAY TODAY® SERIES

THE ULTIMATE SELF-TEACHING SERIES!

How many times have you said: "I wish I would've learned to play guitar… piano… saxophone…" Well, it's time to do something about it. The revolutionary *Play Today!* Series from Hal Leonard will get you doing what you've always wanted to do: make music. Best of all, with these book/CD packs you can listen and learn at your own pace, in the comfort of your own home!

This method can be used by students who want to teach themselves or by teachers for private or group instruction. It is a complete guide to the basics, designed to offer quality instruction in the book and on the CD, terrific songs, and a professional-quality CD with tons of full-demo tracks and audio instruction. Each book includes over 70 great songs and examples!

Play Guitar Today!   DVD 💿 INCLUDES TAB
00696100	Level 1 Book/CD Pack	$9.95
00696101	Level 2 Book/CD Pack	$9.95
00320353	DVD	$14.95
00696102	Songbook Book/CD Pack	$12.95
00699544	Beginner's Pack – Level 1 Book/CD & DVD	$19.95
00842055	Play Today Plus Book/CD Pack	$14.95

Play Bass Today!   DVD 💿 INCLUDES TAB
00842020	Level 1 Book/CD Pack	$9.95
00842036	Level 2 Book/CD Pack	$9.95
00320356	DVD	$14.95
00842037	Songbook Book/CD Pack	$12.95
00699552	Beginner's Pack – Level 1 Book/CD & DVD	$19.95
00698997	Play Today Plus Book/CD Pack	$14.95

Play Drums Today!   DVD 💿
00842021	Level 1 Book/CD Pack	$9.95
00842038	Level 2 Book/CD Pack	$9.95
00320355	DVD	$14.95
00842039	Songbook Book/CD Pack	$12.95
00699551	Beginner's Pack – Level 1 Book/CD & DVD	$19.95
00699001	Play Today Plus Book/CD Pack	$14.95

Play Piano Today!   DVD 💿
00842019	Level 1 Book/CD Pack	$9.95
00842040	Level 2 Book/CD Pack	$9.95
00320354	DVD	$14.95
00842041	Songbook Book/CD Pack	$12.95
00699545	Beginner's Pack – Level 1 Book/CD & DVD	$19.95
00699044	Play Today Plus Book/CD Pack	$14.95

Sing Today!   💿
00699761	Level 1 Book/CD Pack	$9.95

Play Ukulele Today!   💿
00699638	Level 1 Book/CD Pack	$9.95
00699655	Play Today Plus Book/CD Pack	$9.95

Play Alto Sax Today!   DVD 💿
00842049	Level 1 Book/CD Pack	$9.95
00842050	Level 2 Book/CD Pack	$9.95
00320359	DVD	$14.95
00842051	Songbook Book/CD Pack	$12.95
00699555	Beginner's Pack – Level 1 Book/CD & DVD	$19.95
00699492	Play Today Plus Book/CD Pack	$14.95

Play Flute Today!   DVD 💿
00842043	Level 1 Book/CD Pack	$9.95
00842044	Level 2 Book/CD Pack	$9.95
00320360	DVD	$14.95
00842045	Songbook Book/CD Pack	$12.95
00699553	Beginner's Pack – Level 1 Book/CD & DVD	$19.95
00699489	Play Today Plus Book/CD Pack	$14.95

Play Clarinet Today!   DVD 💿
00842046	Level 1 Book/CD Pack	$9.95
00842047	Level 2 Book/CD Pack	$9.95
00320358	DVD	$14.95
00842048	Songbook Book/CD Pack	$12.95
00699554	Beginner's Pack – Level 1 Book/CD & DVD	$19.95
00699490	Play Today Plus Book/CD Pack	$14.95

Play Trumpet Today!   DVD 💿
00842052	Level 1 Book/CD Pack	$9.95
00842053	Level 2 Book/CD Pack	$9.95
00320357	DVD	$14.95
00842054	Songbook Book/CD Pack	$12.95
00699556	Beginner's Pack – Level 1 Book/CD & DVD	$19.95
00699491	Play Today Plus Book/CD Pack	$14.95

Play Trombone Today!   DVD 💿
00699917	Level 1 Book/CD Pack	$9.95
00320508	DVD	$14.95

Play Violin Today!   💿
00699748	Level 1 Book/CD Pack	$9.95

Play Recorder Today!   💿
00700919	Level 1 Book/CD Pack	$7.95

FOR MORE INFORMATION, SEE YOUR LOCAL MUSIC DEALER, OR WRITE TO:

7777 W. BLUEMOUND RD. P.O. BOX 13819 MILWAUKEE, WI 53213

Visit us online at **www.halleonard.com**

Prices, contents and availability subject to change without notice.

0809